Stubble Field

Also by Paul Hunter

One Seed to Another (2010)
Come the Harvest (2008)
Ripening (2007)
Breaking Ground (2004)
Clown Car (2000)
Lay of the Land (1997)
Mockingbird (1981)
Pullman (1976)
Your House Is On Fire and Your
Children Are Gone (1970)

Stubble Field

Paul Hunter

Silverfish Review Press
Eugene, Oregon

ACKNOWLEDGMENTS

With heartfelt thanks to the editors of the following publications, where some of these poems first appeared: *Moving Mountain*: "Plain" and "Slacker." *The Raven Chronicles*: "Providential" and "Scarecrow." *Small Farmer's Journal*: "Slacker," "What the Farm Is," "This Hard Threshing Floor," "The Touch," "Handout," "What They Still Talk About," "Watch Maybe Learn," "Hold Your Horses," "Fanciful," "Sure Sign." *Small Farms Conservancy* website: "Where to Begin." *Northwind Anthology 2010*: "By Way of a Diversion" and "At the Sheriff's Auction." *Windfall*: "The Call."

"Providential" was nominated for the 2009 Pushcart Prize.

"Here and Now" was published as a Wood Works postcard for Winter Solstice 2011.

Abiding thanks as well to those who inadvertently sat for their portraits. Please forgive the author's occasional indiscretion and tacit liberties, lending these lives a voice.

Copyright © 2012 by Silverfish Review Press

Cover photo *Near Quincy* © 2002 by Glenn J. Rudolph

All Rights Reserved
First Edition

This publication was funded in part by a 2012 Publishers Fellowship from Literary Arts of Portland, Oregon.

Published by
Silverfish Review Press
PO Box 3541
Eugene, OR 97403
www.silverfishreviewpress.com

Distributed by
Small Press Distribution
800-869-7533
orders@spdbooks.org
www.spdbooks.org

Library of Congress Cataloging-in-Publication Data

Hunter, Paul, 1943-
　Stubble field / Paul Hunter. -- 1st ed.
　　p. cm.
Poems.
ISBN 978-1-878851-61-1
I. Title.
PS3558.U487S78 2012
811'.54--dc23

2012011134

Manufactured in the United States of America

Contents

I. End of the Road
       Quickstep   9
       Hold Your Horses   10
       Pure Country   12
       What They Still Talk About   13
       What It Would Take   14
       Skeeter   16
       Slacker   17
       Bend That Bow   18
       Scarecrow   20
       Purely by Feel   21
       Past the Point of Turn and Push   22
       Work with Bill   23
       Corn Earworm Crush   24
       By Way of a Diversion   25
       The Touch   26
       Trampling Out the Vintage   28
       Hon   30
       Providential   33

II. Where the Going Gets Rough
       Shucks   37
       Visitation of the Snowy Owl   38
       Plain   40
       Sick   41
       Potshot   42
       Evening Out   43
       How the Business Comes and Goes   44
       Who Took to Farming Right Off   45
       Fanciful   46
       Hard Starting   49
       First Love   50
       Shortcut   52
       Spoiled   54

No Telling   56
Old   59
The Call   61
At the Sheriff's Auction   63
Where to Begin   64
Where the Going Got Rough   65
Come the Winter Rains   66

III. What Leafs Out All Over
Sure Sign   69
Reward Enough the Being Left Alone   70
What the Farm Is   72
How That Works   73
Farm in a Bucket   74
Viking Funeral   76
Watch Maybe Learn   79
At a Glance   80
This Hard Threshing Floor   81
What Still Makes Tracks   82
Where We Stand   83
As if from Plato's Cave   84
Handout   85
Not to Trust   86
Passing Over   87
Here and Now   88
Seeing Our Way Clear   89

Author's Note   91

I. End of the Road

Quickstep

After a long day in the fields
unhitched from whatever it was
worked them into a lather left
standing where tomorrow would begin
plow cultivator jittery mowing machine

Edwin and the team would march along
harness jingling their quickstep
near the barn almost prancing
long reins over his shoulder
furrowing the silky dust behind

as he leans back just enough speaks
so they won't break into a canter
get carried away with him
so in the dark they'll hold still for
the harness lifted wiped down

for them to be turned out
in the twilit yard to roll
before feeding before even
a drink at the stars in the trough
paw the cool air shake the ground

Hold Your Horses

First he taught me how to hold
some carrot or apple
fingers together palm up
because they can't see down past
that velvety nose to their mouth

so the treat even offered
by a harmless eight year old
still might cost a stray nip

then he showed me the bridle
with its steel bit set way back
in the space between their teeth
that could manage them only so far

so you don't want to overdo
and hurt them only then
did he show me how to take the reins
between my thumbs and fingers
to feel in their sensitive mouths
that surge and flow like a river

then finally told me what I need today
is for you to just hold them

so get up close alongside
the tamest of the old boys which is Bill
on a short lead persuade him to accept
that he will have to lift you
clean off the ground to take a step
convince him how much trouble
it would be to dance with you
dangling like a bauble off his chin
though rest assured that he could

he's going to nod and stamp a little
shake his head try to turn and see
back here what I am hitching up
he knows how big he is
likes to show he's impatient
see how much slack you will give
that he can take

but you stand still holding on
convince him with your calm
use both hands make your voice
steady but a little gruff

and even if you still don't half believe
who's boss convince yourself
you'll never lose your grip
let him go do something reckless

Pure Country

Wasn't on the way to anywhere
roads backed up into ruts
dead-ended into foothills between stumps
with only a church and a school
part-time blacksmith gas station mechanic
what any census taker postmistress ag agent
might label pure country

though not so far as the crow flies
from where anybody halfway young
had a hankering to be
towns lit up wide awake
practically through every night
where strangers in mom and pop diners
fed family-style craved entertainment

with ice cream sundaes picture shows
the five and dime antique store auction barn
and for the daring and reckless
after dark the road house honky-tonk
with its strings of blinking lights
its bandstand up over the dance floor
where saxes moaned and guitars wailed

where folks would jump the night out
slosh and nurse their drinks
out under shade trees round the parking lot
fall into clinches and scuffles
do their best and worst to find
themselves something Sunday mornings
to sleep on or wake to regret

What They Still Talk About

Emma's dreamy youngest Jonathan
playing peekaboo with his reflection maybe
looking for the ball of garter snakes
that come springtimes would appear
maybe test that old wives tale to steal a peek
at your future look back in over your shoulder
they never knew exactly what
drew him to the edge tipped him up
pure luck falling didn't break his neck

stuck upside down in the well hollering
lord knows how long like to drowned
till someone thirsty enough
to draw themselves a drink
ran back spread the alarm
then some brave soul had to be found
most likely the one dug the well
to be lowered down their strongest rope
fetched off the barn hay hook
that took all their strength not to drop
onto the boy him and the lantern both

tie the rope to his ankles
draw straight back up the way he went
to deliver to his mother right as rain
like the cork out of a bottle
like the answer that might never come
till everyone planted their feet got a grip
leaned into what had to be done

What It Would Take

One old farmer the elder of the pair
of bachelor Englemann brothers
Herman and Jonathan
mostly law abiding otherwise
never got himself a driver's license
since he'd learned well before
keys in locks started cars
before folks thought of testing
then charging for the privilege of
hand-cranking such a contraption
that might take an arm off
where all day long you'd likely
never see another one
billowing its endless plume of dust
taking your life in your hands
touring backroads these parts

he didn't think of himself
as one more buccaneer
abroad in duster and goggles
oogah horn scattering chickens
spare tires strapped to his turtleback

he was careful at the wheel about
his business never flighty overwrought

and since without the state
so much as lifting a finger
he'd figured what was what
could follow signs and portents
handmade to fit each occasion
more than a trifle irregular
like the big yellow plywood hand
by the schoolyard nailed to a tree
that waved the warning "slow children"

though he never quite learned to read
he caught a little on the fly like Go and Stop
like sewing should a button lose itself
and it wasn't any trouble keeping up
with road changes over the years

but it's not like he never had an accident
there was that cold snap
snow drifting over black ice
slid him sideways off into the crick

and that other time in the pickup
a rock scraped the plug off the pan
blew the engine with a full load on
had to walk home get Jonathan
harness the team to tow in

but Herman never hit a deer or car
exploding out of fog around the bend
would not have said his life was charmed
just didn't much think about
what he got away with sixty years
till late one blazing summer afternoon
he pulled up and parked
in the gravel yard of the Dairy Freeze
where the deputy in his patrol car
not looking backed straight into him

broke out a tail light there they set
had an ice cream cone to cool off
then figured what it would take
Herman to get around
to getting his license at last
written part spoonfed out loud
eye check and road test plus
halfbaked apologies mumbled
between the guilty parties back and forth

Skeeter

Swirling up light as a snowflake
once the mare dropped him
breath caught in his tissues and sticks

so by the time he's licked dry
isn't rickety all set up to be fed
on collapsible legs that would spring
into the air to like Dad said
shake the dust of mortality

maybe any newborn mule
finished before he's begun
fixed from birth with no future
just doesn't want to be hitched
to the day any more than
a boy craves pulling
a wagonload of damp feathers

so inquisitive for the moment
carefree ignorant of rules
lending his long-eared attention
to anything living trailed after
mouse or moth snorting teeth clacking
low to the ground or midair

though in time he would settle
start a load and walk eventually
plod even blindered straight ahead
that first year there was no telling
would he ever grow into his dignity
stand to be harnessed to draw
the life he was meant for
lighthearted shivering leaping
part frog part cricket
part crow part butterfly

Slacker

Your first real job apart from chores
where you spent the day in the field
with the men breaking new ground
with a four-up team of mules

came when Edwin picked out
what he called the slacker
lifted you up on his back on a burlap bag
gave you a long willow switch

told you give him a little
encouragement to keep him pulling
so the whole day long heaving round
you did what you were told

by dark with a raw backside
and a vast appetite for corn fritters
still a little swollen with the pride
being part of the team being trusted

from making that lazy jack work
hitting him on the rump
forcing him to lean into the collar
shouting gruff commands

in the rhythms of your father
giving orders though for once
on the gang plow behind you he sits silent
feels the reins run through his hands

Bend That Bow

Spring field newly plowed
twilight staggering up and down
furrows after what's turned up
like another kind of bird

time we'd always find ourselves
bent down picking rocks
stacking to fill the stone boat
every thaw dislodge aplenty more

Grandpa not bending so easy
takes him a hoe to get after
what he can loosen strike sparks
lean on try and catch his breath

tells about this very time of year
out in this very same field
back when they would tackle
one good stump of a season

that they'd about gotten sick of
zigzag plowing around
fetch axes shovels to surround
the rooted thing reach under

far as you can dig cut free
then flatten off the one side take
log chain to tie on and spike
a twenty-five-foot hickory pole

hitch the team the far end walk
the big boys around bend that bow
hold your breath to hear way down
about to bust that tearing sound

let fly maybe take off an ear
like happened to great-uncle Bud
till you twist that tap root clean off
unscrew up out of the ground

and finally pitch dark now drag clear
and till call to wash up for supper
start to fill that hole invisible
hardly counted working any more

Scarecrow

Crows don't scare so easy
in among the swelling corn they love
or bowlegged strolling our garden
clacking snipping savoring
a strawberry a ripe grape
we appear to have raised just for them

at vast distances they recognize
a gun identify whoever uses one
penetrate an overcoat disguise
a limp that conceals a murderous intent
spot the pickup that rolls down a window
to offer its muzzle a long shot

so when there does appear
a fluttering ragged suit of clothes
a human form set to stand guard
over all we've planted round the clock
he may serve to frighten
milder flightier less reprehensible hordes

but for the dark brethren
who study and know us who surround
our doings with their surveillance
their chuckling embellishments
their occasional derision
their deft and absolute theft

this gang demands
nothing short of the real thing
children with stones in their pockets
for several weeks paid to defend
from the likes of such brazen marauders
our ripening outstanding cherry tree

Purely by Feel

Jimmy's first real job was delivering milk
for an old farmer who'd worked up a little route
through town and back to the farm before
anyone but the paper boy woke up

this farmer deathly afraid of fire
wouldn't have a lantern in the barn
so Jimmy learned how to harness
the horse in pitch dark purely by feel

when he asked where the milk route ran
the farmer pointed to the mare
said you just head her into town
she knows right where to turn

and where she stops you look up
on the porch and if there's two
empties then you leave two
four means four whatever they put out

since the Depression hung on hereabouts
first of the month he'd leave an envelope
pick up next morning whatever it contained
handful of pennies or whatnot

the old man never would complain
said he was too tired to go around
in daylight counting kids to see
who had most need of his milk

said long as he could grow his hay and oats
milk his old gals in the dark
afternoons maybe catch a little nap
by and by it would likely all add up

Past the Point of Turn and Push

Her basket of doorknobs
all porcelain or tarnished brass
kept in the woodshed where
hens would never find by accident
hanging up there on a nail
brood on the whole damn pile

where on the way to feed
and gather in she'll duck
slip one in her apron pocket
for the hen too troubled
today by her endless thefts
unable to rest easy so upset

by the hand stealing warm eggs
out from under her clutch
that at last this substitute
might be offered the poor dear
a tranquilizer to hatch
something eternal to polish

Work with Bill

Six days a week in all weather
his long shadow off to one side
did what I was told stood dumb
in return hardly having to shoulder
the worry with him working alongside

most times could hardly measure
the effect of what we did
would crouch there stretching fence
as the rain would overtake us
strain the come-along aquiver

while he leaned in pounded steeples
punctuating the thought
at least we'll get one more post
before we're drenched to the skin
no place to run to anyhow

no hurry packing our tools
to make a beeline for the shed
to lug in wipe down oil put away
then after evening chores maybe go
light a fire to stand slowly turning before

Corn Earworm Crush

For days after he showed me
how they bored in the silk of
the young ears beginning to come on
ate all that was tender and secret

I would walk a corn row each morning
headed down the road toward Bill's
providing I weren't late for work
pick off each corn earworm crush

the tiger-striped thing in my fingers
that could bend around pinch you
back pretty good with those jaws
wipe their juice on my pants

which Bill would notice finally ask
if I was fixing them all one by one
like the old folks did the hard way
in their spare time with a laugh

said there was aplenty more
of them than us then wondered if
I saw one et by anything perchance
some bird we might offer a bounty

By Way of a Diversion

Now and then a peddler passing through
drummer tinker rambling handyman
through Saturdays on into supper
out front of the general store would set
on the bench unlimber and tune up

while folks would draw nigh and linger
till there'd be a considerable hearing
for whatever he had to offer
throw in some beans bread and coffee
trade you for a decent team of mules

carpenter who'd bend his Swedish saw
into an S he'd stroke with a fiddle bow
pour out a waltz of pure silver
or hand come haying time who plucked
a mandolin or mean banjo

cut a buck-and-wing we'd memorize
for winter nights we only had ourselves
catch on the fly every motion
might help to piece it together
work through kinks and fits to recollect

for that time after dinner dishes
when out would come the rattletrap
gitfiddle with its rusty slackened strings
that still might be coaxed to remember
half a cripple creek or wildwood flower

The Touch

Though most worked off to themselves
pritnear all the folks studied
some trick of their own to fall back on

got known for doing far and wide
what looked natural as falling off a log
like one old boy could tie a grain sack knot

quick as a cat at spilt milk
one could shuck a dried corn ear
spill a gold twist in his hat

like wringing a young chicken's neck
some could stir fire in a woodstove
boil coffee up a couple seconds flat

and talk of secret recipes who'd dare
bring cornbread to the potluck
if Rosalie felt up to baking hers

everyone could sharpen axes knives
though stropping razors to a fare-thee-well
came like pie to the storekeep

some could worry through a certain tune
on the squeeze box or gitfiddle
that most never quite got the hang of

a few could do sums in their head
some cooking never measured out a thing
seemed like what they threw together

would always land about perfect
some ventured nothing but a grin
a knack for the kind word when needed

but none expected dinner to appear
without their lifting a finger
or a song to start up on its own

that not a soul could remember
and canning snap beans rolling pie crust out
shingling a hip roof never leak a drop

should anybody run into a hitch
they'd wrack their brains to recollect
who hereabouts could do what needed done

go ask for help admit they had the touch
and sure would be applauded going at
what no one else could figure out a lick

Trampling Out the Vintage

Late summers Edwin between crops
would go along through his arbor
pick and barehanded crush grapes

let them work in the crock
siphon from carboy to bottle
cork and stack and let set

then past the first of the year with
precious little left to worry out-of-doors
go around visit three-four friends

who also trampled out the vintage
as they liked to call it though
none used their feet in these parts

they'd blow the dust off old bottles
set out every glass and jelly jar
back and forth swap New Year's toasts

taste how theirs did alongside his
as they all knew there would be
good years and bad sweet and puckery

sips of the dark ruby stuff
but that they'd get better at it
providing they took care kept clean

same time didn't use too much soap
overlook some green or shriveled fruit
that there is always such a thing as luck

that left years to age in the cellar
like the chair of a painless dentist
time takes the bite out

till the bad turns more than passable
held up these cold nights to lamplight
in every face the hopeful wine aglow

Hon

Dawn of the day they'd arrive
all the cousins nephews nieces
for the midsummer picnic out-of-doors
on the farm he was born to
Hon would be first up for chores
milk and feed livestock that done
arrange tables of sawhorses planks
benches all around and kitchen chairs

then try to help stir in the pantry
be shooed away by the family
the brother his wife and their kids
who never would ask him to do
anything that's beyond him
no saying grace no killing chickens
so to pass the time find him a job
cutting flowers spreading tablecloths

from the first he knew things
rough and loud here had no place
at the worst could hurt others' feelings
with his size and booming voice
so mostly labored to appear
small enough and quiet
though in an instant he could mock
any grownup yammer and strut
have to leave the room to calm himself

but then after all this piling up
spreading out neatening and more
all at once here they are
exploding into the open
out of crowded shiny overheated cars
every one bigger than last year
in their bright kid hair and clothes

brandnew yet familiar
their secret whispers and smiles
young and old greeting him
using his own grownup name
though the family still calls him Hon
his mother's pet name in his crib
recalling how long she's been gone

from these mingled generations rollicking
through this balmy open-ended day
with no reminders how he never
marched away to war in uniform
never slow-danced with the girls
he couldn't quite learn the point of

and today appointed farm ambassador
leading the children of old playmates where
he proudly shows off kittens baby pigs
climbs the fragrant haymow for the view
warns about the weary mama sow
the touchy dairy bull in his corral

and later in the shade the cooling air
as the creaking tables quiet down
after mountains of dinner
handcranked ice cream cakes and pies
watermelon from the spring house sliced
to eat along the fencerow spitting seeds

in the endless summer twilight
where men his age have returned
to the heave and clank of the horseshoes
where they puff stogies by the damp clay pits
sip last year's homemade wine
while women climb the porch to set
in the afterglow rock and gossip

comes time to play his favorite hide-and-seek
in the yard he's mown and raked
with the old dog barking after
one then another crouching out of sight
telling on them all can't help herself

till the seeker sings out olly olly ox in free
and with long hair streaming they appear
fleet as young deer dodging bounding
all run tag the ancient maple tree

then mason jars to capture lightning bugs
and pitchdark at last lanterns lit
sparklers waved aloft a blinding scribble
checkers spilling out along the table
any last amusement to delay
the moment of leavetaking when

this same grown middleaged child
who never more than faintly understood
how one by one they leave off playing
grow up and strike out on their own
with him left standing outside
as if at the door of first grade

might hold a daylong playmate by the hand
muss the tangled hair the sleepy head
maybe pinch or tug a little
then linger in the dark yard wave
through the slow pop and crunch of the gravel
as the laden car breaks free and pulls away

Providential

Every Sunday morning they file in
this tiny wooden church all painted white
men's hair wetted down neatly raked
about to curl back up
women's glory gathered under hats

fill in the last row on forward
so whenever latecomers appear
in whatever harried condition
shuffle to the empty seats down front
the earlybirds get to watch

study someone you might never otherwise
settled in this quiet service where
no surprise how often things occur
you dasn't dare laugh at
seem almost providential

like when Elmer sits down on his hat
Aunt Emma passes the gas
for the umpteenth time the minister
goes to tell that bible salesman joke
like his sermon's forgive and forget

and delivering a homily should all else fail
the cat will get after a fieldmouse
life and death askitter underfoot
or sparrow chased by nothing
batter up against the colored glass

II. Where the Going Gets Rough

Shucks

Every summer come wheat harvest
the moment would arrive to drag
old mattresses out in the sunshine
dump damp moldy guts on the compost
stuff the ticks full with new straw

and every year all over hear tell how
where Pa grew up back in the hills
for bedding outhouse what have you
all they had was corn shucks
rustle should you chance to move a muscle

never mind wiping your backside
good for scouring the skillet
with that cob to feed the woodstove
shocks of whatall heaped aplenty
like to never rot and springy tough

so folks would lay still while they slept
else wake one and all like us kids
when the bedbugs get something awful
even asleep commence to thrash around
like a brandnew married couple

till got so Grandma would get up
go through the medicine bottles
stuff cotton into everybody's ears
so we'd all quit shouting quiet
and the tiredest at least could drop off

Visitation of the Snowy Owl

During the first windstorm
that tore away soaked and pasted
the last of the rustling leaves
rattled every wooden skeleton

when we'd about settled for
a winter of more of the same
slumped in the shivering dark
ornery plain colorless

daybreak in the crest of the sycamore
knotted bulging with age Grandma said
slept with its foot down our well
we looked up there it was

agleam against the dull sky
hurting our hooded eyes
twice as big as any hereabouts
the size of a polar bear cub

with an icy unblinking stare
that saw clean through us overlooked
the farm till not even Grandma is sure
exactly whether scourge or patron saint

that wide awake there swaying sat
through the stormy day to drop down once
where we'd cooped the hens up
caught and shredded a field mouse

watched all through that moonlit night
sighing beyond our drawn curtains
till the wind died with dawn lifted off
circled low then vanished white on white

and wherever else it might visit
whoever whether blessed or cursed
that pale archangel of the tundra
at least once its cold stare had picked us

Plain

One bright fall morning Grandma wove
her a corncob doll the old way
unpainted unadorned

its rough red body bound
tight in a dampened shuck dress
that would end in outstretched arms

her plain shuck face round and open
but for three thumbnail dents featureless
with a shuck kerchief gathered around

the braids of her long silken hair
that caring for over that winter
would grow ever paler and finer

Sick

She made sure there was plenty cooked
breakfast in the kitchen steaming hot
saw the men safely off to the field
kids bundled out to the bus
toting sack lunches and homework

took laundry down off the line stiff
wrestled it more or less flat
then posted chores for the oldest
the moment she'd walk in from school
headed straight to the fridge for a snack

changed a diaper wiped a runny nose
on the littlest in her playpen
then climbed in bed pulled covers up
like sputtering snow on a stovetop
said now take the day to be sick

Potshot

Because they cleaned cooked
and ate what they hunted fed
a table full of hungry little ones
through lean years filled the cookpot
one family considered to be theirs
all the small game in these parts

forget licenses fencelines bag limits
the week before fall season opening
the Rafferty boys before daylight
then again around twilight would stalk
every woodlot and pasture sweep along
every wandering treelined crick

on their self-appointed rounds
methodical efficient silent merciless
take what squirrel rabbit pheasant opossum
woodchuck quail they had a mind to
toy balloon stretched over the muzzle
potshot each with a muffled .22 short

then burdened bound home for the freezer
take turns lug the one bloody sack
where every road sign in their passing
read aloud in the dark for effect
No Hunting No Trespassing Posted
drew another deadly parting shot

Evening Out

Meese's underfed cattle like
to get out down along the crick
slip under the wire at one bend
wade into deep new grass
in the neighbors' bottomland

though he is slow to round up
at fence-mending sloppy and slack
who can begrudge them the mouthful
you'd have to be blind not to notice
their shambling bones sticking out

so the neighbors are of the opinion
old man Meese should be jailed
for running cows on his upland
that fatten no more than pigs fly
at least make the effort to quiet

the skinny dogs he keeps chained up
when you are forced to come by
because he won't answer his phone
where you both know the longer he stalls
the more living his cows will come home

How the Business Comes and Goes

Despite scarce jobs and money tight
hope humming in the air before the war
what with their firstborn come due

they built a fancy new outhouse
with two holes one large one small
a little step for climbing to the throne

with lids so a grownup could sit
alongside the little one show how
to answer the call of nature as it were

lend a hand croon encouragement
with a high window so they could see
maybe read a favorite picture book

take time to visit make a little game of
learning how the business comes and goes
so when the little ones grew

big enough not to fall through
every once in a while for old time's sake
the smaller hole would secretly get used

Who Took to Farming Right Off

With a plow neatly fashioned
by an older brother of a mangled kitchen knife
a harrow with its teeth of roofing nails
a disk strung up of flattened bottle caps
by the kitchen door he scoured and scratched
till pebble-free he had a silky patch
fine as any field the grownups worked

then planted what they did for crops
in tiny rows a little soybeans wheat corn oats
that in a week or so came up
looked about perfect three days
to be weeded and watered and played with
then his plants proceeded to reach up
dwarf his toys crowd one another out

Fanciful

Old neighbor farmer Briggs would happen by
after supper dishes oftentimes
set on the porch toward sundown
whittling his crookback walking stick
hand around a sack of horehound drops
bribing us kids to sit quiet
suck while he commenced to tell about
the pair of bats in his barn the other night
made such a squeaky racket deaf or drunk

they put him in mind of a horse he had once
who'd sit on his tail like a dog
beg for beer in a bucket and how
he once had a Poland China sow
could count to seven or nine but not eight
that wintered up under his house
that not even the bull pup could fetch
dug into the root cellar there
ate him pritnear out of raw turnips
though she got to like em best cooked
in a cream sauce with green peas

but mostly liked to tell about his cows
since we lived down a valley mostly flat
with his ground higher up above
what he called a mountain couple hills
where he said his cows grazing there
would grow two longer legs on one side
to keep em on a level sorta like
and how they'd have to corkscrew
around and around to the top
where starting home then some got stuck

like that pair of identical baby goats
Esmeralda hatched once Pete and Repeat
mostly called Little Sir Echo
since Pete as the firstborn was boss
liked to chase squirrels off the woodshed
then stand up there scared to jump off
crybabies whining all night long
though they'd find a way down to breakfast

but where was I now those cows
had to back down the whole way
they climbed up step by step
else coming round the dark side
of the mountain might forget
which foot they started out on
commence to lean out like to fall
thataways clean to the bottom
like one winter they had one black cow
tumble down something awful
took to calling her Snowball

but if they wasn't too old
or broke all their legs had to be
put out of their misery
their mommas might just take pity
finally teach em right
to know which side was what
lean into that hill not away
take it a step at a time till eventually
come down second nature smooth as pie

and should any kid giggle or cough
roll their eyes make as if to plug their mouth
he'd point up the side of the mountain
show how their perfect little trails
weaving into and out of each other
never went straight up and down
like a dumb new state highway
but sensible always took the long way round

till by the end he'd have to make
the kids go ask their momma if
whatall he said weren't the gospel
watch her planted in the doorway serious
holding onto herself something fierce
say Mr Briggs may sound a little fanciful
but they do things different
in that thin air way up where he's from
so behooves us to show some compassion

Hard Starting

The kid who saved up bought
that whizzer motorbike
behind his parents' back
praying for the perfect time
to ask if he could keep

hid it in the woodlot where
the road would turn and dip
just past the neighbors' pasture
whose small boys without being told
right off read its whole story

went after chores twice a day to lift
the scrap of canvas study never touch
spoke in its presence in whispers
would have had their tongues
cut out to keep its secret

though something in them knew
no thing this loud and fast
with rusty tank and tubes all painted blue
dented chrome tailpipe bruised purple
mushy tires with hardly any brakes

gently wiped wherever it leaked oil
that took such peddling like hell
to mount that rugged uphill slope
with them all pushing running alongside
anything so hard starting

still so beautiful and true
could he get it once to catch
would roar burn its belts and spray gravel
turn heartless that instant and leave them
flopping in its dust its distant past

First Love

When Ethan appeared after school
to help Angelina with chores
even the little ones knew
from their stiff silent dance

something was up just not what
though they could see
clear from the henhouse
he wasn't helping with theirs

and after that first teasing chant
shushed by their mother they
noticed their sister was given
a job away off in the orchard

where through that fall
planting the ladder with
the greatest possible care
he'd help her clean every tree

they'd take turns catching
the apples the other would toss
down then sort in four baskets
for market eating pie and cider

precise as any grownups
finally gather windfalls for the pigs
where sleepy yellowjackets still abuzz
in their moldy frostbitten cores

would draw her small O of surprise
that he would mirror steadying
her on tiptoe long and lean
kerchief round her flowing hair

contained reaching out overhead
where he dreamt of catching her falling
kept his eyes up his feet planted
as she with eyes averted would bestow

on him from her apron pocket
the best ripest one from each tree
perfect for his dark walk home
for his personal eating

Shortcut

Late walking home from the dance
pitch dark without moon or stars
joking as we grope our way along
the shoulder where weeds meet gravel
from one barnyard light to the next
dawdle till approaching the shortcut
through woodlot and pasture
that saves an easy couple miles
we turn off downhill locate the gate latch
by feel take twenty steps into trees
that close in around like a cave like
the insides of a black cow underground

where the air is cool and still
not a breath stirs not a sound
but leaves underfoot crunch and rustle
branches claw at faces brushing past
as we stumble and stagger till the first
one stops the rest blunder into behind
in a knot stand quiet till the last
wonders have we gotten off the path

so we figure not to make it worse
check our pockets no one has a match
asked who can halfway see to lead
no one has the faintest inkling
from here there's no telling we're lost

which up till now had always been a game
where each would seemingly dissolve
into the friendly night then sneaking back
give others a fright poke a shout
but that was on the summer lawn
with a good fence all around
mown smooth and soft as a carpet

so here we stand take one anothers' hands
like kindergarteners hushed to hear
a hoot owl call away somewhere
underfoot hear something fearful scurry off
politely ask which way we think
we came till all agree at least it was
uphill from here then slowly turn
touching arms outstretched to stalk

no telling what we may hit first a stump
then shagbark hickory then sticker bush
feel our prickly way till blessed fence
bites each of us in turn sent sidling
together to the gate to find ourselves
set brave and noisy once more on the road
resigned to take the longer way around

Spoiled

Along the porch of an evening
they still like to tell on how Marie
her first job babysitting
hardly more than half a child herself
going to change diapers
threw up all over the baby
consider the verdict unanimous
she'd never had to dig enough manure
that sure would like to have toughened her

Marie not a blister or callous
Marie studious quiet lyrical
never a hair out of place
devout patient mindful effortless
kind word or deed for anyone who asked
what boys these parts would call a natural
though to her face they'd say spoiled

who'd congratulate themselves
for knowing she would get
all she could handle and more
from the common pigyard fund of excrement
when she got in the family way
seventeen disowned compelled to settle for
a hardscrabble place away back in the hills
skinny fool with his dirty hands full
and no truck with politeness
took to calling her princess

still the boys love best
these tales of her early comeuppance
told over like they really can't recall
what was beside the point
or could turn back the clock

to that picnic somehow once Marie
got the bumblebees in her hair
had to jump in the frog pond
turned her lacy dress all green
stank with the slime that
the rest of the day stuck to her

No Telling

Late one Saturday I wandered
through leaves drifting toward fall
to poke around maybe see
were the fox squirrels fattening
hard to spot so secret purely wild
ten more days till season opening

with no gun so as not be tempted
just enough of an evening breeze
so they'd be up and moving
as I crept around the woods to where
nut trees would be sure to draw them
white oak beechnut walnut hickory

but then further back on the rise
through dappled shade a sudden hard surprise
four stumps dipped in gold
four tulip poplars four longstanding lives
now sawdust splashes bright wedges
acres of limbs and strewn topping

dents in a clearing what's left
fence flattened rusty snarls torn free
where a logging truck had swung in
turned around to drop the trees
one at a time winch the logs up
chain the heavy load and steal away

I doubled back through woods to go tell Bill
who would be setting rocking by the radio
his shoes already kicked aside
who'd jump up struggle back into those shoes
hardly tie before he'd fetch some tools
to mend fence till dark and wait supper

even with no cattle in these woods
I'd seen Bill often set off in a whirl
for him there would be no rest
till you'd fixed a thing gone wrong
did what you could to set right
even here where the trees were not his

he would have phonecalls to make
to the owner and sheriff invite
whoever wants to come out have a look
count and measure take pictures to show
whatever there was left behind to see
on top of which Bill would ponder

how the neighbors when their cows got loose
could come round act so polite
yet turn a deaf ear such loud business
he'd wonder where we'd even gone so long
the thieves got the notion there'd be
time enough to buck and haul those trees

then he'd recall it must have been
the county fair we'd spent all day
a couple weeks back taking in
which a man is entitled to a taste of
once a year not be made to suffer for
fancy roosters in a cage some peanut brittle

or was it poor Ron Wyler's funeral
that they'd held the potluck after
where nobody wanted anyone to leave
and worry it till even a good man
would be up to his eyeballs in doubt
no way of telling anything for sure

but the price of a log of grade-A poplar veneer
that had been robbed in broad daylight
with nothing to be done to make it right
so already good and tired resolved
to tell Bill Sunday morning save myself the walk
take our one good chance a week to sleep in late

Old

Watching his grandad at dinner
fork chase the final cold
green bean round the plate
locate his tentative mouth

fumble his key in its lock
poke and turn blindly to where
it encounters a few good teeth
gets worried swallowed at last

that night bone-tired starts to think
with all the young round the place
plumped and trundled to market
what does it mean growing old

an eternity that single swayback mule
kept to till the garden Jezebel
lightfoot still watches her step
whose age nobody rightly can recall

he thinks of endless babies come in waves
calves and piglets lambs and chicks
almost too many to notice
the handful that fall by the way

he remembers when the dairy bull got slow
nothing left to him but a bawling nudge
one morning loaded and gone next day
another thickneck rears and snorts

so mostly how the living seem to go
hardly frisky a minute then a few
hang on a dog's age a coon's age
or barn cats a yawn all their lives

and laying there he wonders whether old
includes this mattress where he finds
himself slumped into a crater broken down
by all those heavy sleepers gone before

The Call

Ellie thought she'd gotten far enough
away from the farm beyond college
settled down career in management
lease on a highrise potted coffee plants
business-cut designer suit matching
necklace and earrings briefcase and high heels

so when the call came come quick
poor Dad fell down suffered a stroke
eighty-six now this looks to be it
she was set for the bedside talk holding hands
hall conferences the whispering among
doctors nurses orderlies round the clock
but then drove straight from work
to the old home place where they said
she was needed they're desperate

and met at the front door first thing
the sister who lived up the road
on the corner lot she'd been given
said you've got to do something with the girls
they haven't been milked in thirty-six hours
and all of the milkers are broken

she knew her dad's way with machines
that he couldn't fix exactly but
could tweak and tinker and coax
a thing back from the grave
hum a little say a soothing word
over whatever he's stuck on
somehow wake it up
not with a kick and a curse
said tantrums don't amount to much
only make a thing worse

but for all his useless pleasantries
not one of them could figure out
the trick to his jury-rigged wiring
not the boys and neither of the girls

so she went in her parents' bedroom
shut the door stripped down past pantyhose
to put on her dead mother's clothes
still heaped in drawers hung on hooks
bloomers flannel workshirt overalls
never mind how they fit two pairs of socks
stuffed in her black rubber boots
went out got a pail
washed and warmed up her hands
to start in milking
the one way she knew how
all twentythree of those cows
two of whom remembered her for sure

and in a year there she was
past another funeral
feeling both empty and full
with the old man's soothing phrases
humming again on her lips
back managing the dairy farm as if
she was the one never left
who couldn't pretend to forget
the call they all learned to answer
before they knew what it meant

At the Sheriff's Auction

They go through the old place
like a buzz saw late one blinding
cold Saturday morning
corral all around the auction block

buzzards clamped on the top rail
scanning mangy livestock
pick through every rusty bit laid out

big stuff goes for nickels on the dollar
one ton Ford flatbed hundred and a half
worn-out Cockshutt combine a couple
Deering parts mowers you could maybe
make into one good one
hardly pay to haul off

scour through the barnyard
pantry then cellar then attic
nest of castiron skillets
case of canning jars
look to be still full of pickles
sink all the way down to the last
selling gates off the hinges
what am I bid for solid steel nine total
all the same price buyer's choice

so when the gavel bangs
they leave the place wide open
sign who could care less
what might wander through
this land from here on out
maybe never turn again to make a crop

Where to Begin

Each generation the farm
has to be started over
as the land is handed down
you pause look where to begin

pencil a cardboard scrap
head-down stalk figuring
whatall has usually been
waiting to be carried on

then calculate what might be
ask yourself why not
rearrange a thing or two
dam that crick for a pond

tear out the barn partitions
for the new young team
take up chickens again
or let go the bother

as hardly worth your while
reckon you'll maybe move
the garden for better daylight
on around to the south

wait for inspiration
but not a minute too long
asking whatfor you could get
stuck in a daydream walk off

lose yourself a decent couple years
leaving the fields alone
turn and what's standing there
saplings thick as your arm

Where the Going Got Rough

Out past our village crossroads where
all the back roads were gravel
rutted humpbacked broken up
like to shaken loose
your final wisdom tooth

the County Road Superintendant
like he was lord of the turnpike
with golden keys to the bank vault
had the road paved to his door

Buzz Buckley that bull of a man
so-called for the no-nonsense haircut
a rarity those shaggy times these parts
who in conversation led with
his forehead like a concrete block
with two little glittering eyes
like mica stove windows
set back in the shadows underneath

that to hear him tell it worked
a hundred hours a week
the odd blizzard emergency
landslide round the clock

and even when he got sacked
for what the papers termed "peculation"
taking that truckload of rock salt
meant to give us all traction
home to feed his own cattle
that blacktop so easy so slick
still stopped at his place to remind us
right where the going got rough

Come the Winter Rains

Some joy to see the loss of their effect
overnight in the still of one pristine
snowfall on the fallow land
that softens the familiar filling in
each scribble of the work each arabesque

yet winter can bring on a troubled sleep
a heaving back and forth
a giant laid to rest the troubled earth
that at the touch of sunlight stirs
and stretching all its dark limbs reaches up

even so toward either end will come
that moment full skies open for
a hammering incessant dull downfall
that swamping chastening soaks in
until exhausted flooded fields dissolve

where your life wakens regardless
rain drumming your thin skin
half-naked in the dark you find yourself
with the cows out some tree down
some break in the fence to be mended

with no shred of comfort out-of-doors
having lost that first lesson of living
to dress for the weather or suffer
where come the winter rains the driven
pour of chilled shot rattling shingles

come the stark set of the jaw nailed shut
the upturned collar shivering the sodden
shoes that founder gasping in their pools
the way it keeps bucketing down
soon as not you'll likely catch your death

III. What Leafs Out All Over

Sure Sign

Hens patrolling for bugs
argue over the weather

swallows swoop as one
vast wing upswept to feed
on the wave of what's coming

a hillside of cattle lie down
tails to the wind a sure sign

and practically last to notice
crickets urgently stammer
to anyone who will listen
get that wash off the line

Reward Enough the Being Left Alone

Among the fields we work in turn
this one has grown somehow favored
for the angle of the low spring sun
that catches and warms it
how the mist encircles its fencelines
how it holds the downhill runoff

yet dries out firms up earliest
to let us get into and work
right when we need to begin
to feel useful and shake off
the drowsy winter's plodding shivering
burn to put seed in the ground

that set back furthest from the road
allows nobody passing to admire
what's poking up leafing out
see how we're getting on much less
turn jealous what looks from a distance
to scarce amount to anything just yet

though with a smattering of clues
a bird house every other fence post
with its lyrical outspoken sentinel
straw to mulch the row crops
and along fences lush undergrowth
bees in wildflowers delirious

and now with hard red winter wheat and hay
grown together both finished
that fine clover-timothy mix
its leaf curl and fragrance cured perfect
that calves appear to more than tolerate
for its sunny taste down the darkest of days

having yielded us the finest corn and beans
now wheat and hay in living memory
delivered all we could ask of
a soil crumbly and fine as ancient cheese
dark as a moonless night past the first of the year
drowsing fragrant expectant

around the kitchen table it's agreed
our favorite has earned a rest a fallow year
with the stubble left to hold
a place for what's to come
reward enough the being left alone
through another winter slumber

What the Farm Is

The farm is not its barn nor house nor shed
nor tractor wagon horses oxen mules
not hay nor seed corn not its workshop tools
not canning jars nor graveyard for its dead

but land grown used to working down the years
its rolling open fields its acreage
some left in pasture woods along each edge
where crops leave off where wilderness appears

and all we do in time what's gathered in
is weighed against what's waiting to be done
yet farming doesn't waste a mouthful where
what molders by the way or in the bin
is shoveled under spread around the one
abundance always craving some repair

How That Works

Out by the road at a bend a wide flat spot
they put up a roadside stand
whitewashed boards slanted tables
roofed over once lightning had split
the great shade maple living eighty years
alongside gravel and mud before blacktop
that in summer dust made the place feel
less of a business more of a picnic spot

still invites you to slow down pull in
where some things never change
where to an invisible distant tractor stutter
lost in green fields shimmering in the heat
one pesky yellowjacket guards the fruit
a pile of paper bags flutter under their rock
where a hanging scale sways
needle aquiver weighing every breath

and all around boxes and baskets offering
whatever's in season and ripe
then too honey piccalilli barbecue in jars
every item its handlettered price
rusty cash box bolted down with a slot
cigar box of change with a sign alongside
reads Honor System you know how that works
please pay for whatever you take

where chances are you'll get to meditate
spend time considering what you'd like
peel back and finger sweet corn lift
and wonder what to make of crookneck squash
in midair let it do a little dance
without so much as a smile or how-do
from those with work aplenty off doing it
most likely with no one in sight

Farm in a Bucket

When the country boy retires
not from a lifetime of farming
but from that hard start
sleeping in the chicken shed
age eight to sixteen
killing scalding plucking
three hundred a weekend
grown up to do anything but

coming out the other side
of the tunnel of his life he sells
that fine house sick of its acres
of old trees lawn and rose garden
fireplace big enough to roast an ox
where nights he'd poke logs swirl a drink
wad and burn up his memories

and when they moved it was like
he died went up to heaven
penthouse nineteenth floor
183 feet from solid ground
measured his first night with
a crescent wrench a ball of string
and his own wingspan

with a warm dry underground garage
would keep the Buick forever
with powder blue cloud carpets where
a country boy might kick away his shoes
wander about his eyrie

but with no fireplace to feed
his crumpled late night thoughts
just a chute to rattle down empties

maybe to keep himself
reaching up not letting go
his first spring day the new place
all of a sudden he drags up
what he calls his farm in a bucket
some whiskey barrels cut in half
some bags of expensive dirt
to plant tomatoes sweet corn
bell peppers pole beans whatnot

set out along his balcony
that with a northwest exposure
do about like you'd expect
spring up like weeds
then summer storms and winds
batter half to death
make him run to the hardware
that stays open late
keep him out in the dark with
flashlight stapler lathe heavy plastic
that would flap till it split
sail away downwind for miles

that he would keep wrestling with
get up out of bed to check
try his damnedest to protect
those green handfuls of living
so rare so high up
that in the end a pale taste
is all they can offer him back

Viking Funeral

You don't blame the watering hole
for what you pour down yourself
and the Five Spot is that kind of place
of a late afternoon where a guy
ducks in for a beer takes a stool
offers up his problem one and all
turn to like fresh pizza flopped
on the bar they're suitably inclined
to help him chew while it's warm

so Larry's Percheron workhorse Prince
lay down nothing more to be done
but sit on the ground hold his head
the first one he'd known his whole life
that he'd handraised from a colt
that couldn't quite wait for the vet
who was off pushing through drifts
to bring a little hope to someone else
so after a while let him go
and but for spreading the tarp
that seemed a decent minimum
couldn't think where to start

so the bartender cracks the phone book
hears the rendering truck has to come
from the next county over hears $130
which nobody has in these parts
which calls for another round
Larry says he'd bury him himself
but for the hard frozen ground
someone suggests dynamite
maybe can spare a few sticks
which hardly seems fitting and proper
then someone thinks what everyone
still has piles around this time of year

brush they could build up a bonfire
burn the poor thing down to ash
taking the memories with it
stately as a Viking funeral

which no one around here has tried
but sounds enough like a plan
that Larry can head home
next morning several neighbors come
help pile a couple wagonloads of brush
on the dead horse sprinkle kerosene
then touch the whole thing off ker-woosh
that flares up ten minutes then dies
singes the hair off poor Prince
darkens his pale sorrel hide
raises a bit of a stink but
doesn't begin to make a dent
in that hump on that hillside

so next day word spreads far and wide
from the Five Spot twenty wagon loads
of brush half a dozen cords of wood
piled up thirty feet high
this time get the job done

and when it gets touched off again
old truck tires a gallon of gas
the smells both cooked and rotten
go traveling downwind for miles
and after a short day long night
of it blazing off in the pasture
that draws the volunteer
fire brigade for a look
still that giant horse won't disappear
when the fire slumps down
everyone can tell the blackened thing
split open like rust a dark red

lies where he fell on his side
stretched out straight
his four legs his iron shoes
his elegant long neck and head

at which point Larry notices
the ground all round him feeling soft
as if the hillside has thawed
thinks maybe to bury at last
goes to start his frontend loader
coming downhill lowers the bucket
as if to lift that big boy up
out of his smoldering bed

but then the loader starts to sink
into the spot where the fire
its glowing mountain of coals
floats on a muddy swamp
and as it topples Larry flutters free
dumbfounded quivering watches
his tractor catch fire and sputtering
slide down underneath the horse
as if to go to bed and wait for spring
to come back and bury what's left

Watch Maybe Learn

When your horse lies down that last time
when you can't coax her back with
a carrot stout pull at her halter
can't get down behind to help lift her
call out her name in that gruff
weary voice that means business
that somehow always used to raise her up

now toward the end join the others
the silent ones standing around
watch what they do maybe learn
how some hover fearful to come close
some can't help their needing to approach
nudge at her know it's no comfort
some make as if to graze and turn away

some even run a little ways
from whatever has stricken her
then double back to rejoin
whatever seems to sit on her
patient as a vulture all the day
holding her head down eyeing her
breathing as it roughly comes and goes

At a Glance

This fall one grizzled neighbor stacks
spare hay in his old boxcar
by the barn on concrete blocks
some years what's been a corncrib
granary what have you says it holds
the overflow what needs to sit and wait
past New Year's turn a profit

says it only cost three hundred bucks
what with the moving and calking
weathertight best deal he ever made
like to have a whole trainful
on the place stacked up
some way else they could get to look
like all them what you call it trailer parks

course you can even be too practical
says something in him always wished
he'd kept the couplers wheels and trucks
that went for scrap if only to say at a glance
from back in its traveling days what started out
though it won't budge again what it was for
how it made the million miles to here

This Hard Threshing Floor

Within where the great door stands open
but for storms three seasons of the year
empty claw of a hay fork planted
rotten rope still rove to spare a climb

uneven worn smooth hoof-scarred
this hard threshing floor
despite gloom and barn litter
underfoot gleams eternally bright

still lends a spring to the step
no wonder here have been dances
around behind great beasts that trampled
what others outside winnowed in the wind

no picturesque reminder
how they did such things before
but held in reserve a prime tool
once built set in place like a law

in extremity should it be needed
all else fail still as rope and pail
by the well spade and sickle by planting
no finer footing maybe even now

What Still Makes Tracks

Up the pasture trail to the spring
set back among hills the farmer stops
at a pawprint like none he has seen
huge slowmoving sharp-clawed definite

that because nobody would believe
what ranges in this close unless
having looked after most of a lifetime
saw for themselves what broke cover

expect to never see here now much less
snap pictures near absolute proof
so he trudges home to get the stuff
to kneel down in the mud and pour a cast

to keep up on the mantel show around
glad of any chance to answer back
whoever says what these woods held
and lost say look what still makes tracks

Where We Stand

Underfoot overhead though they touch
there is something indeterminate
to their stand how trunks go up
silvery some forty feet before
the first green outburst catches
below that false starts shaded out

still days I often think a tree
lives on as nothing but itself
only somewhere to stand
somehow to reach down
something to hold onto and hold up
belonging alone no offering

but then in a gust company
recalls how we learn to love
where we stand shoulder to shoulder
imperceptibly turn to the sun
without seeking forgiveness
crowd out one another

sometimes in a high wind in damp
uncertain footing like to topple
we might crave to stand apart
though more likely even then
we would lean in our feathery heads
spin and sway fall to dancing

As if from Plato's Cave

In his branching tunnels the mole
samples grubs and worms a connoisseur
erupts in our finest croplands but prefers
the vain green lawn we mow
and preen for nothing we could name

where even the young dog in daylight
cannot stop his exuberant spilling forth
that the farmer in his rocker would allow
is practically worthless to bother
with his pink nose backward claws
what's left of eyes sunk in velvet

blindly running his burrows we wonder
why he takes chances to surface
is each crater a chase ended badly
a cul-de-sac for his dumptruck
an explosive touch of claustrophobia

all this dazzle may be beyond him
yet something in him is driven
to leap like a fish out of water
plunge like a bird in the ocean
like a man drawn out past midnight
immerse in a sky gushing stars

Handout

Hard-handed sunburnt folks of few words
liked to say you get what you got coming
in the end pritinear what you deserve
could even sound a touch heartless

but then offer neighbors the handout
of seed corn they could count on
a prime cow worth the milking
not some windbag aflutter on the breeze

but the shirt off their own back where
they had felt the bloody stroke of trouble
planted themselves to lean into the wheel
or turned from the storm run for cover

and at the worst in the field on one knee
would pray for rain a long slow soaking one
without wind on its heels or sun before
though they'd take and like whatever come

Not to Trust

Some say don't name the ones
you plan to eat though the same
ones say they don't have feelings
which you'd have to be
made of stone not to see

how they know not to trust us
with the most elemental things
take a young cow bred
for the dairy or beef herd
in her wrenching first labor

takes watching keeping her close
she'll want to steal away
to a thicket the end of the pasture
have her baby there all to herself
no matter how it hurts

how confused overburdened lost
hide from us till she feels
well enough to stagger back around
show off this tiny new life
given to her not to us

Passing Over

These evenings geese flying south
their dark skeins and threads
pulled apart wound together
in the pale air passing over

shuffle positions and trade
leaders every few miles
let someone younger and stronger
battle a way to the front

share the fatigue the despair
breaking through this blind chill
to scout a safe landing
settle for rest frozen fodder

identical plaintive their calls
scattered over the shoulder
announce the position of each
repeat what those drawn after

must help every leader remember
have to know and keep knowing
by endless persistent reminders
how all are meant to arrive

Here and Now

A stretch of storms and we begin to feel
like twigs torn away by the winds
like leaves flattened and stuck
to what matters dead underfoot

we figure autumn practically defunct
summer a distant fleeting memory
but then slogging out to the barn
sky breaks open all at once we see

in a shaft of sun a swarm of midges
like minnows that flash down a well
like a spangled constellation so remote
still dancing its one here and now

Seeing Our Way Clear

No matter this morning
fog holds us close
with chores to do anyhow

nothing much to look at
pitchforks in the calf pen
mucking out underfoot

until midmorning haze
burns off heads lift as day
breaks open all at once we see

clear across the valley where
out ahead of a rattling pickup
the road climbs out of sight

the one way to get anywhere
from here just now that
we don't need to take

Author's Note

These farming poems began in relentless recognition that the ways that made me were gone. Without regrets or apologies I looked for the source of my values, sought to deflate some easy myths, reassure myself at midlife how I knew what worked, what was lasting right and wrong. But vinelike in season the poems have grown into an extended metaphor, not of a world that used to be, but of a world that's ongoing.

Another book followed, and another, on account of things left unsaid and undone. In each case the work found a shape that could stand alongside the others. Immersed in the working round of field and barn, woodlot and pasture, I'd forgotten how much of a role the social whirl played in the country, for all the isolation, especially where women fit in. And the more I looked, the more I felt the sweep of my family's century and a half in a region that I hope feels close to one you have known.

Savoring the length and depth of time on the land, I came to realize that as stories arise, often with hardly a hitch despite the reach from dirt-floored cabin to suburban manicure, that old farming world and its values are far from done. With the onslaught of industrial agriculture, those folks may have hunkered down, but were not beaten out of existence. Despite denial, dismissal, excuses, the next generation of farmers comes sputtering awake to find itself anew with its work and reward near at hand.

The interior text and display type as well as the back cover text were set in Adobe Jenson, a faithful electronic version of the 1470 roman face of Nicolas Jenson. Jenson was a Frenchman employed as the mintmaster at Tours. Legend has it that he was sent to Mainz in 1458 by Charles VII to learn the new art of printing in the shop of Gutenberg, and import it to France. But he never returned, appearing in Venice in 1468; there his first roman types appeared, in his edition of Eusebius. He moved to Rome at the invitation of Pope Sixtus IV, where he died in 1480.

Type historian Daniel Berkeley Updike praises the Jenson Roman for "its readability, its mellowness of form, and the evenness of color in mass." Updike concludes, "Jenson's roman types have been the accepted models for roman letters ever since he made them, and, repeatedly copied in our own day, have never been equalled."

The title on the cover was set in Poetica. Designed in 1992, Poetica was modeled on chancery handwriting scripts developed during the Italian Renaissance. This elegant style of writing formed the basis for italic typefaces and for modern calligraphy. The author's name was set in Gilgamesh. The work of British designer Michael Gills, Gilgamesh is based largely on his calligraphic experiments and is named after a poem from Middle Eastern mythology, "The Epic of Gilgamesh." Gilgamesh offers functionality with style and will give emphasis to any typographic design.

Silverfish Review Press is committed to preserving ancient forests and natural resources. We elected to print *Stubble Field* on 30% post consumer recycled paper, processed chlorine free. As a result, for this printing, we have saved: 1 tree (40' tall and 6-8" diameter), 499 gallons of water, 293 kilowatt hours of electricity, 64 pounds of solid waste, and 120 pounds of greenhouse gases. Thomson-Shore, Inc. is a member of Green Press Initiative, a nonprofit program dedicated to supporting authors, publishers, and suppliers in their efforts to reduce their use of fiber obtained from endangered forests. For more information, visit www.greenpressinitiative.org.

Cover design by Valerie Brewster, Scribe Typography.
Text design by Rodger Moody and Connie Kudura, ProtoType Graphics.
Printed on acid-free papers and bound by Thomson-Shore, Inc.